contents

getting started

There are more than 100 delicious recipes for panini, wraps, rolls, and sandwiches in this book. Almost all of them are simple and require only basic skills and a few minutes to prepare. All recipes have been rated for difficulty: 1 (simple) or 2 (fairly simple). In these pages we have chosen 25 of the most enticing recipes, just to get you started!

● SIMPLE

CHEESE, SALAMI & ARUGULA wraps

CHICKEN, SLAW & PAPAYA wraps

PLOUGHMAN'S wraps

CUCUMBER & TAPENADE sandwich

SALMON, MASCARPONE & LIME rolls

ARUGULA, TOMATO & GOAT CHEESE panini

CHEESE & CARAMELIZED ONION panini

● VEGETARIAN

ROASTED BELL PEPPER & HUMMUS wraps

CURRIED TOFU wraps

EGG & CHEESE baguette

CLASSICS

CLASSIC REUBEN
panini · 36

FALAFEL & HUMMUS
wraps · 77

CAPRESE *panini* · 26

TUNA & MAYONNAISE
rolls · 104

PARMA HAM & BUTTER
sandwiches · 96

CHEESE, CUMIN
& GOLDEN RAISIN *panini* · 18

TUNA & PESTO
wraps · 87

EDITOR'S CHOICE

SALAMI & FRESH FIG
sandwiches · 101

ROBIOLA & SMOKED
SALMON *rolls* · 106

HOT STUFF CHICKEN *sourdough panini* · 32

BEST FOCACCIA

TOMATO & MACKEREL
focaccia · 91

BEST PANINO

PROSCIUTTO & SUN-
DRIED TOMATO *panini* · 17

BEST BREAD ROLL

GRILLED MUSHROOM
rolls · 94

BEST WRAP

MEATBALL & BABA
GANOUSH *wrap* · 91

BEST SANDWICH

SPICY PROVOLONE &
GREEN APPLE *sandwiches* · 109

panini

ARUGULA, TOMATO & GOAT CHEESE panini

2	squares plain focaccia (about 8 inches/20 cm each)
1	clove garlic, peeled but whole
4	ounces (120 g) creamy fresh goat cheese, such as chèvre or caprino
	Small bunch arugula (rocket)
12	cherry tomatoes, halved
12	leaves fresh basil, torn
1–2	tablespoons extra-virgin olive oil (optional)
	Salt and freshly ground black pepper

Serves 2 • Preparation 10 minutes • Cooking 5–10 minutes • Difficulty 1

1. Preheat a sandwich toaster or panini press on medium-high heat.

2. Split the focaccias in half horizontally. Rub the garlic clove over the bread so that it is perfumed but not stinky with garlic.

3. Spread one half of each focaccia with goat cheese. Cover with the arugula, tomatoes, and basil. Drizzle with the oil, if using, and season with salt and pepper. Cover with the remaining pieces of focaccia.

4. Toast until the focaccia is crisp and golden brown and the filling is heated through, 5–10 minutes. Serve hot.

If you liked this recipe, you will love these as well.

FIG, PANCETTA & GOAT CHEESE panini

CAPRESE panini

SUN-DRIED TOMATO & CHEESE panini

The word panini is Italian for "sandwiches," but in many parts of the world it has come to mean "toasted sandwiches." In this chapter all the panini are toasted. There are many good sandwich toasters and panini presses available and most are reasonably priced. We suggest you use one of these to make the panini. If you don't have one, don't give up! Panini with flat slices of bread and non-bulky fillings can be cooked in a lightly oiled frying pan, griddle, or grill pan. Press down with a metal spatula to brown, then carefully flip and cook the other side. Panini made with baguettes or bulky rolls and fillings can be cooked in a toaster oven or regular oven at about 400°F (200°C/gas 6) until golden brown and heated through.

PANCETTA & PINEAPPLE sesame panini

1	tablespoon extra-virgin olive oil
1	medium onion, sliced
2	white sesame or whole-wheat (wholemeal) bread rolls
4	thick slices pancetta (or prosciutto or ham)
1	small clove garlic, finely chopped (optional)
4–6	tablespoons finely chopped fresh pineapple or well-drained crushed canned pineapple
1–2	tablespoons sweet chile sauce, storebought or homemade (see page 10)
	Freshly ground black pepper

Serves 2 • Preparation 10 minutes • Cooking 5–10 minutes • Difficulty 1

1. Preheat a sandwich toaster or panini press on medium-high heat.

2. Heat the oil in a frying pan over medium-high heat and sauté the onion until softened, 3–4 minutes.

3. Cut the rolls in half and spread with the onions, pancetta, garlic, and pineapple. Drizzle with the sweet chile sauce and season with pepper.

4. Toast until the rolls are crisp and golden brown and the filling is heated through, 5–10 minutes. Serve hot.

If you liked this recipe, you will love these as well.

MORTADELLA, CHEESE & SALAD panini

PROSCIUTTO & SUN-DRIED TOMATO panini

SPICY SALAMI, OLIVE & GARLIC panini

SWEET CHILE sauce

Makes about 2 cups (500 ml) • Preparation 10 minutes + 12 hours to cool • Cooking 15–20 minutes • Difficulty 1

1¹/₂	cups (300 g) sugar	1	teaspoon finely grated ginger
1	cup (250 ml) rice wine vinegar	1	clove garlic, finely chopped
¹/₂	cup (120 ml) water		
2	large red chiles, thinly sliced		

1. Combine the sugar, rice wine vinegar, and water in a medium heavy-based saucepan over high heat and bring to a boil. Decrease the heat to low, add the chiles, ginger, and garlic and gently simmer until reduced by half, 15–20 minutes.

2. Set aside to cool for 12 hours before using.

3. Store in sterilized glass bottles or jars in the refrigerator for up to a month. Refrigerate after opening.

KETCHUP

Makes about 3 cups (750 ml) • Preparation 15 minutes + 12 hours to cool • Cooking 15–20 minutes • Difficulty 1

2	(14-ounce/400-g) cans chopped tomatoes, with juice	1	clove garlic, minced
¹/₂	medium onion, grated	2	bay leaves
2	tablespoons sugar	2	juniper berries
2	tablespoons cider vinegar	3	whole cloves

1. Put the tomatoes in a food processor and blend until smooth.

2. Place the tomato purée and the onion, sugar, cider vinegar, garlic, bay leaves, juniper berries, and cloves in a medium heavy-based saucepan over high heat and bring to a boil. Decrease the heat to low and gently simmer until thickened to sauce consistency, 15–20 minutes.

3. Pass the sauce through a fine-mesh sieve, discarding any solids. Pour into sterilized glass bottles or jars and refrigerate overnight before use.

4. Store in the refrigerator for up to a month.

GREEN OLIVE tapenade

Makes about 1 cup (250 ml) • Preparation 5–10 minutes Difficulty 1

1¹/₂	cups (250 g) pitted green olives	3	anchovy fillets, coarsely chopped
¹/₂	cup (15 g) flatleaf parsley leaves	1	tablespoon freshly squeezed lemon juice
2	cloves garlic, coarsely chopped	3	tablespoons extra-virgin olive oil
1	tablespoon salt-cured capers, rinsed		Salt and freshly ground black pepper

1. Combine the olives, parsley, garlic, capers, and anchovies in a food processor and pulse until coarsely blended. Add the lemon juice and gradually pour in the oil, blending to make a smooth paste. Season with salt and pepper.

2. Use immediately or store in an airtight container in the refrigerator for up to one week.

SMOKEY BARBECUE sauce

Makes about 3 cups (750 ml) • Preparation 15 minutes + 12 hours to cool • Cooking 20–30 minutes • Difficulty 1

¹/₄	cup (60 ml) extra-virgin olive oil		packed brown sugar
1	medium onion, finely chopped	¹/₄	cup (60 ml) Worcestershire sauce
3	cloves garlic, minced	2	teaspoons liquid smoke
2	(14-ounce/400-g) cans chopped tomatoes, with juice	1¹/₂	teaspoons chile powder
		1	teaspoon mustard powder
¹/₃	cup (90 ml) malt vinegar	1	teaspoon ground cumin
¹/₄	cup (50 g) firmly	¹/₂	teaspoon Tabasco sauce

1. Heat the oil in a medium heavy-based saucepan over medium-low heat. Add the onion and garlic and sauté until golden, about 5 minutes.

2. Add the tomatoes, malt vinegar, brown sugar, Worcestershire sauce, liquid smoke, chile powder, mustard powder, cumin, and Tabasco sauce. Stir to combine and bring to a boil. Decrease the heat to low and simmer until thickened, 20–30 minutes.

3. Pour into sterilized glass bottles or jars and refrigerate overnight before use.

4. Store in the refrigerator for up to a month.

PECORINO, HONEY & WALNUT *panini*

4 slices walnut bread or firm-textured (homestyle) white or brown bread

4 ounces (120 g) pecorino (or Parmesan) cheese, in flakes

12 walnuts, toasted and broken into pieces

2–3 tablespoons honey

Serves 2 • Preparation 10 minutes • Cooking 5–10 minutes • Difficulty 1

1. Preheat a sandwich toaster or panini press on medium-high heat.

2. Cover two slices of bread with flakes of pecorino. Top with the walnuts and drizzle with the honey. Cover with the remaining slices of bread.

3. Toast until the bread is crisp and golden brown and the cheese is melted, 5–10 minutes. Serve hot.

FIG, PANCETTA & GOAT CHEESE panini

4   thick slices firm-textured (homestyle) white or brown bread

3   ounces (90 g) fresh, creamy goat cheese, such as chèvre or caprino

      Small bunch arugula (rocket), chopped

      Salt and freshly ground black pepper

4   slices pancetta (or salami)

4   fresh figs, halved

Serves 2 • Preparation 10 minutes • Cooking 5–10 minutes • Difficulty 1

1. Preheat a sandwich toaster or panini press on medium-high heat.

2. Spread two slices of bread with the goat cheese and top with the arugula. Season with salt and pepper. Arrange the pancetta and figs on top and cover with the remaining slices of bread.

3. Toast until the bread is crisp and golden brown and the filling is heated through, 5–10 minutes. Serve hot.

13

Mortadella, also known as Bologna sausage in English, is a delicately flavored luncheon meat from the central Italian city of Bologna. Made with pork, it has whole grains of black pepper which flavor the meat during the long, gentle steaming process. Substitute with a high-quality local luncheon meat if preferred.

MORTADELLA, CHEESE & SALAD panini

2	large white bread rolls
4	tablespoons (60 g) mayonnaise, storebought or homemade (see page 42)
1	cup (50 g) salad greens
4	ounces (120 g) mortadella, thinly sliced
4	ounces (120 g) Gruyère (or Swiss or Cheddar) cheese, thinly sliced
6-8	cherry tomatoes, halved or sliced
	Salt and freshly ground black pepper

Serves 2 • Preparation 10 minutes • Cooking 5–10 minutes • Difficulty 1

1. Preheat a sandwich toaster or panini press on medium-high heat.

2. Split the rolls in half and spread the mayonnaise on the bottom half of each roll. Cover with a layer of salad greens. Top with the mortadella, cheese, and tomatoes. Season with salt and pepper. Cover with the top half of each roll.

3. Toast until the rolls are crisp and golden brown and the cheese is melted, 5–10 minutes. Serve hot.

If you liked this recipe, you will love these as well.

PANCETTA & PINEAPPLE
sesame panini

**ITALIAN SAUSAGE
& ONION** panini

**MUSHROOM, BACON
& PESTO** panini

CHICKEN, CELERY & PISTACHIO panini

4   thick slices whole-wheat (wholemeal) or white toast bread

2–3   tablespoons mayonnaise, storebought or homemade (see page 42)

4   ounces (120 g) roast chicken, sliced

1   stalk celery, thinly sliced

2–3   tablespoons pistachio nuts, shelled and toasted

      Salt and freshly ground black pepper

Serves 2 • Preparation 10 minutes • Cooking 5–10 minutes • Difficulty 1

1. Preheat a sandwich toaster or panini press on medium-high heat.

2. Lay the slices of bread on a work surface. Up end a bowl about 3 inches (8–10 cm) in diameter and use it to cut out rounds.

3. Spread the bread with mayonnaise. Cover two rounds with chicken and top with celery and pistachios. Season with salt and pepper. Cover with the remaining rounds of bread.

4. Toast until the bread is crisp and golden brown and the filling is heated through, 5–10 minutes. Serve hot.

PROSCIUTTO & SUNDRIED TOMATO *panini*

2   thick slices eggplant
    (aubergine), with skin
2   round five-grain bread rolls
2   large slices mozzarella cheese
2   large thin slices prosciutto
    (or ham)
4   sundried tomatoes, chopped
    Freshly ground black pepper

Serves 2 • Preparation 10 minutes • Cooking 10–20 minutes • Difficulty 1

1. Preheat a sandwich toaster or panini press on medium-high heat.

2. Grill the slices of eggplant in a preheated grill pan over high heat until tender, 5–7 minutes.

3. Cut the bread rolls in half and cover with the eggplant and mozzarella. Fold the prosciutto over the cheese and top with the sundried tomatoes. Season with pepper. Cover with the top halves of the rolls.

4. Toast until the bread is crisp and golden brown and the cheese is melted, 5–10 minutes. Serve hot.

Cumin and cheese go very well together, especially when accompanied by sweet golden raisins (sultanas). If liked, replace the golden raisins with another dried or candied fruit, such as cranberries, ginger, pineapple, or papaya. You can also replace the Gruyère with another cheese, such as Gouda, Cheddar, or Fontina—just be sure to choose one that has plenty of flavor.

CHEESE, CUMIN & GOLDEN RAISIN panini

2	round walnut bread or white or whole-wheat (wholemeal) rolls
2-4	tablespoons mayonnaise, storebought or homemade (see page 42)
2	teaspoons Dijon mustard
4	ounces (120 g) Gruyère (or Swiss or Fontina or Cheddar) cheese, thinly sliced
2-3	tablespoons golden raisins (sultanas)
1	teaspoon cumin seeds

Serves 2 • Preparation 10 minutes • Cooking 5-10 minutes • Difficulty 1

1. Preheat a sandwich toaster or panini press on medium-high heat.

2. Cut the rolls in half and spread with the mayonnaise and mustard. Cover with the cheese and sprinkle with the golden raisins and cumin seeds. Cover with the top halves of each roll.

3. Toast until the bread is crisp and golden brown and the cheese is melted, 5–10 minutes. Serve hot.

If you liked this recipe, you will love these as well.

PECORINO, HONEY & WALNUT panini

SUNDRIED TOMATO & CHEESE panini

CHEESE & CARAMELIZED ONION panini

ITALIAN SAUSAGE & ONION *panini*

2 tablespoons extra-virgin olive oil

2 large white onions, sliced

2 large Italian sausages

2 long firm-textured (homestyle) white or whole-wheat (wholemeal) bread rolls

4–6 tablespoons ketchup or smokey barbecue sauce, storebought or homemade (see page 10)

Serves 2 • Preparation 10 minutes • Cooking 10–20 minutes • Difficulty 1

1. Preheat a sandwich toaster or panini press on medium-high heat.

2. Heat the oil in a medium frying pan or grill pan over medium heat and sauté the onion until soft and lightly golden, 4–5 minutes. Set aside.

3. Cut the sausages in half and cook in the same pan until nicely browned, 5–10 minutes.

4. Cut the bread rolls in half and cover with a layer of onions. Top with the sausage and the remaining onions. Drizzle with the ketchup. Cover with the tops of the rolls.

5. Toast until the bread is crisp and golden brown and the filling is heated through, 5–10 minutes. Serve hot.

SPICY SALAMI, OLIVE & GARLIC *panini*

2   squares plain focaccia (about 8 inches/20 cm each)

2   large ripe tomatoes, sliced

3   ounces (100 g) thinly sliced spicy salami

2   cloves garlic, thinly sliced

4   large black olives, pitted and coarsely chopped

2   tablespoon finely chopped fresh oregano (or flat-leaf parsley)

2   tablespoons extra-virgin olive oil

     Salt and freshly ground black pepper

1. Preheat a sandwich toaster or panini press on medium-high heat.

2. Split the pieces of focaccia in half. Cover the two bottom halves with slices of tomato and salami. Top with the garlic, olives, and oregano. Drizzle with the oil and season with salt and pepper. Cover with the top pieces of focaccia.

3. Toast until the focaccia is crisp and golden brown and the filling is heated through, 5–10 minutes. Serve hot.

If short of time, use well-drained storebought canned or bottled roasted eggplant and bell pepper.

22

GRILLED VEGGIE & PESTO panini

1	red bell pepper (capsicum), sliced
1	small eggplant (aubergine), sliced, with skin
1	zucchini (courgette), sliced lengthwise
	Salt
2	tablespoons extra-virgin olive oil
$1/2$	cup (120 ml) pesto, storebought or homemade (see page 42)
2	ciabattas (about 3 x 8 inches /8 x 20 cm each)
1	tablespoon finely chopped fresh mint

Serves 2 • Preparation 15 minutes • Cooking 15–25 minutes • Difficulty 1

1. Preheat a sandwich toaster or panini press on medium-high heat.

2. Season the bell pepper, eggplant, and zucchini lightly with salt. Drizzle with the oil. Cook in a grill pan over medium-high heat until tender and marked with black lines, 10–15 minutes.

3. Split the ciabattas open and spread the two bottom halves with a layer of pesto. Cover with the grilled vegetables and mint. Drizzle with the remaining pesto. Cover with the top halves of the ciabattas.

4. Toast until the bread is crisp and golden brown and the filling is heated through, 5–10 minutes. Serve hot.

If you liked this recipe, you will love these as well.

CAPRESE panini

GRILLED MUSHROOM rolls

GRILLED VEGGIE focaccias

TURKEY, BELL PEPPER & HAZELNUT panini

4   large thick slices firm-textured (homestyle) white or brown bread

4   tablespoons (60 ml) mayonnaise, storebought or homemade (see pages 42)

2   teaspoons Dijon mustard

4–6   pieces well-drained storebought roasted red bell pepper (capsicum)

4   ounces (120 g) thinly sliced roast turkey

4   tablespoons hazelnuts, toasted and coarsely chopped

    Salt and freshly ground black pepper

Serves 2 • Preparation 10 minutes • Cooking 5–10 minutes • Difficulty 1

1. Preheat a sandwich toaster or panini press on medium-high heat.

2. Mix the mayonnaise and mustard in a small bowl. Spread the mayonnaise mixture on two slices of bread. Cover with the turkey and bell pepper. Sprinkle with the hazelnuts and season with salt and pepper. Cover with the remaining slices of bread.

3. Toast until the bread is crisp and golden brown and the filling is heated through, 5–10 minutes. Serve hot.

CHEESE & BACON rye panini

4   large thick slices rye bread
4   ounces (120 g) thinly sliced Emmental cheese
2–3   large slices bacon (or pancetta), rinds removed
1   small clove garlic, finely chopped
     Freshly ground black pepper

Serves 2 • Preparation 10 minutes • Cooking 5–10 minutes • Difficulty 1

1. Preheat a sandwich toaster or panini press on medium-high heat.

2. Cover two slices of bread with the cheese and top with the bacon. Sprinkle with the garlic. Season with freshly ground black pepper. Cover with the remaining slices of bread.

3. Toast until the bread is crisp and the cheese is melted, 5–10 minutes. Serve hot.

This sandwich is named for the famous salad that comes from the beautiful island of Capri, off the coast of Naples in southern Italy. Be sure to use top-quality *mozzarella di bufala* (water buffalo mozzarella) or another fresh mozzarella cheese and not the mozzarella made for pizza. You will also need best-quality extra-virgin olive oil and fresh basil.

CAPRESE panini

1	long baguette (French loaf) (or ciabatta)
5	ounces (150 g) fresh water buffalo mozzarella cheese, sliced
2	medium tomatoes, thinly sliced
1	teaspoon dried oregano
	Fresh basil leaves
	Salt and freshly ground black pepper
1–2	tablespoons extra-virgin olive oil

Serves 1–2 • Preparation 10 minutes • Cooking 5–10 minutes • Difficulty 1

1. Preheat a sandwich toaster or panini press on medium-high heat.

2. Split the baguette in half. Cover the bottom half with the slices of mozzarella and tomatoes. Sprinkle with the oregano and basil leaves. Season with salt and pepper and drizzle with the oil. Cover with the top half of the baguette. Cut in half so that it will fit in the toaster.

3. Toast until the bread is crisp and golden brown and the filling is heated through, 5–10 minutes. Serve hot.

If you liked this recipe, you will love these as well.

ARUGULA, TOMATO & GOAT CHEESE panini

SPINACH & PROVOLONE WRAPS with pesto

TOMATO & ARUGULA baguette

If cooking the chicken for this sandwich, see the instructions for poaching chicken breasts on page 60. You can also use smoked chicken or turkey slices in these panini.

28

CHICKEN, FETA & PESTO panini

2	squares focaccia (about 8 inches/20 cm each)
1/2	cup (120 ml) pesto, storebought or homemade (see page 42)
1/2	cup (50 g) kalamata olives, pitted and coursely chopped
2	tomatoes, thinly sliced
20	leaves baby spinach
5	ounces (150 g) feta cheese, sliced
1	cooked chicken breast, sliced or about 8 ounces (250 g) leftover grilled or roast chicken
	Salt and freshly ground black pepper
1–2	tablespoons extra-virgin olive oil

Serves 2 • Preparation 10 minutes • Cooking 5–10 minutes • Difficulty 1

1. Preheat a sandwich toaster or panini press on medium-high heat.

2. Cut the pieces of focaccia in half. Spread the bottom halves with pesto. Cover with the olives, tomatoes, spinach, feta, and chicken. Season with salt and pepper and drizzle with the oil. Cover with the top pieces of focaccia.

3. Toast until the bread is crisp and golden brown and the filling is heated through, 5–10 minutes. Serve hot.

If you liked this recipe, you will love these as well.

16
CHICKEN, CELERY & PISTACHIO panini

24
TURKEY, BELL PEPPER & HAZELNUT panini

32
HOT STUFF CHICKEN SOURDOUGH panini

SUNDRIED TOMATO & CHEESE panini

¼ cup (50 ml) fresh creamy goat cheese, such as chèvre or caprino
¼ cup (50 ml) ricotta cheese
¼ teaspoon dried oregano
4 large slices sourdough bread
1 tablespoon extra-virgin olive oil
1 cup (50 g) baby spinach leaves
4–6 sundried tomatoes, drained and coarsely chopped
2 ounces (60 g) Parmesan cheese, in shavings
Freshly ground black pepper

Serves 2 • Preparation 10 minutes • Cooking 5–10 minutes • Difficulty 1

1. Preheat a sandwich toaster or panini press on medium-high heat.

2. Mix the goat cheese, ricotta, and oregano in a bowl.

3. Brush one side of each bread slice with oil. Place two slices on a work surface, oiled-side down, and spread with the goat cheese mixture. Top with the spinach, sundried tomatoes, and Parmesan. Season with pepper. Cover with the remaining pieces of bread.

4. Toast until the bread is crisp and golden brown and the filling is heated through, 5–10 minutes. Serve hot.

ROAST BEEF & BALSAMIC ONION *panini*

1   small red onion, thinly sliced

Salt and freshly ground black pepper

5   tablespoons (75 ml) balsamic vinegar

2   ciabatta bread rolls

4   ounces (120 g) sliced roast beef

6   cherry tomatoes, sliced

Fresh basil leaves

Serves 2 • Preparation 10 minutes + 1 hour to marinate • Cooking 5–10 minutes • Difficulty 1

1. Preheat a sandwich toaster or panini press on medium-high heat.

2. Put the onion in a small bowl. Season with salt and pepper and cover with balsamic vinegar. Let marinate for at least an hour.

3. Cut the ciabatta rolls in half. Cover with a layer of roast beef, tomatoes, and basil. Drain the onion and arrange on top. Drizzle with the balsamic marinade. Cover with the top layers of the ciabatta rolls.

4. Toast until the bread is crisp and golden brown and the filling is heated through, 5–10 minutes. Serve hot.

Tasty sourdough bread contains a lactobacillus culture which gives it its signature tangy flavor. Sourdough goes well with chicken and also with chile making these panini winners every time.

HOT STUFF CHICKEN sourdough panini

3	ounces (90 g) pancetta, cut in small cubes
4	slices sourdough bread
$\frac{1}{2}$	cup (120 ml) Caesar Dressing
1	cooked chicken breast (about 5 ounces/150 g), diced
1	cup (150 g) freshly grated Cheddar cheese
1	red chile, seeded and finely chopped
1	tablespoon coarsely chopped fresh cilantro (coriander)
2	tablespoons melted butter

Serves 2 • Preparation 10 minutes • Cooking 5–10 minutes • Difficulty 1

1. Preheat a sandwich toaster or panini press on medium-high heat.

2. Put the pancetta in a small frying pan over medium heat and sauté until crisp and golden brown.

3. Spread one side of each slice of bread with Caesar Dressing. Place the chicken on top of two slices, sprinkle with the cheese, pancetta, chile, and cilantro. Cover with the remaining slices of bread. Spread the outsides of the bread with the butter.

4. Toast until the bread is crisp and golden brown and the filling is heated through, 5–10 minutes. Serve hot.

If you liked this recipe, you will love these as well.

SWEET & SPICY CHICKEN wraps

CHICKEN & BELL PEPPER wraps

TANDOORI CHICKEN & YOGURT WRAPS

ROASTED APPLE & CHEESE panini

2   Granny Smith apples, cored and sliced into thin wedges

8   slices cinnamon raisin bread

4   ounces (120 g) Brie cheese, sliced thinly

4   tablespoons pecan halves

Serves 4 • Preparation 10 minutes • Cooking 20–25 minutes • Difficulty 2

1. Preheat the oven to 400°F (200°C/gas 6).

2. Lightly oil a baking sheet and arrange the apples on the sheet. Bake for 15–20 minutes until the apples are soft and golden brown with a caramelized crust on the bottom.

3. Preheat a sandwich toaster or panini press on medium-high heat.

4. Set out four slices of cinnamon raisin bread. Top with cheese, roasted apple slices, and pecans. Top each sandwich with another slice of bread.

5. Toast until the bread is golden brown and the cheese is melted, 5–10 minutes. Serve hot.

SOURDOUGH CHEESE & CHUTNEY *panini*

8 slices sourdough bread

8 large slices sharp cheddar cheese

About $1/2$ cup (120 g) tomato chutney, storebought or homemade (see page 42)

Fresh cilantro (coriander) leaves

4 tablespoons (60 g) butter, at room temperature (optional)

Serves 4 • Preparation 10 minutes • Cooking 5–10 minutes • Difficulty 1

1. Preheat a sandwich toaster or panini press on medium-high heat.

2. Set out four slices of bread and spread each one with 1–2 tablespoons of chutney. Top with two slices of cheese and sprinkle with a few cilantro leaves. Top each sandwich with another slice of bread.

3. If liked, butter the outsides of the bread.

4. Toast until the bread is golden brown and the cheese is melted, 5–10 minutes. Serve hot.

A Reuben panini has layers of meat (either corned beef or pastrami), sauerkraut, Swiss cheese, and dressing between thick slices of rye bread. According to legend, it was invented in New York in the 1920s by Reuben Arnold, the proprietor of the famous Reuben's Delicatessen. The deli no longer exists, but the sandwich lives on.

36

CLASSIC REUBEN *panini*

8	slices rye bread
1/4	cup (60 g) melted butter
1	cup (250 ml) Thousand Island Dressing
8	slices Swiss Cheese
1	(14-ounce/400-g) can sauerkraut, well drained
8	ounces (250 g) corned beef, thinly sliced

Serves 4 • Preparation 10 minutes • Cooking 5–10 minutes • Difficulty 1

1. Preheat a sandwich toaster or panini press on medium-high heat.

2. Brush one side of each slice of bread with a thin layer of melted butter.

3. Turn four slices of bread over and spread with the Thousand Island Dressing. Top with Swiss cheese, sauerkraut, and corned beef. Cover with the remaining slices of bread, butter-side out.

4. Toast until the bread is crisp and golden brown and the filling is heated through, 5–10 minutes. Serve hot.

If you liked this recipe, you will love these as well.

25

CHEESE & BACON
rye panini

31

**ROAST BEEF &
BALSAMIC ONION** panini

39

**MUSHROOM, BACON
& PESTO** panini

ROASTED MUSHROOM & MOZZARELLA *panini*

4-6 medium white mushrooms, stems removed

Salt

2 tablespoons extra-virgin olive oil

$^1/_2$ cup (120 ml) storebought or homemade green olive tapenade (see page 10)

1 long baguette (French loaf), cut in half lengthwise and then in half again to make 2 sandwiches

8 ounces (250 g) fresh mozzarella cheese, sliced

1 cup (50 g) watercress

Serves 2 • Preparation 10 minutes • Cooking 15–20 minutes • Difficulty 1

1. Preheat the oven to 450°F (225°C/gas 7). Put the mushrooms in a baking pan and season with salt. Drizzle with the oil. Roast until soft and the edges turn brown, about 10 minutes.

2. Preheat a sandwich toaster or panini press on medium-high heat.

3. Spread the tapenade on the bottom pieces of the bread. Lay the mozzarella slices over the top. Put the mushrooms over the cheese, and finish with the watercress. Top with the remaining pieces of baguette.

4. Toast until the bread is crisp and golden brown and the filling is heated through, 5–10 minutes. Serve hot.

MUSHROOM, BACON & PESTO panini

8   slices white, brown, or corn toast bread

¼   cup (60 g) melted butter

½   cup (120 g) pesto, storebought or homemade (see page 42)

1   cup sliced white mushrooms

½   cup (120 ml) Caesar Dressing

8   ounces (250 g) shredded mozzarella cheese

12   slices cooked bacon

2   tomatoes, sliced

¼   teaspoon freshly ground pepper

8   large fresh basil leaves

Serves 4 • Preparation 15 minutes • Cooking 5–10 minutes • Difficulty 1

1. Preheat a sandwich toaster or panini press on medium-high heat.

2. Brush one side of each slice of bread with a thin layer of melted butter. Spread four slices of bread with the pesto and set aside.

3. Spread the remaining four slices of bread with the Caesar Dressing. Top with mozzarella, bacon, mushrooms, and tomatoes. Season with pepper and add the basil leaves. Top with the pesto slices (pesto-side down).

4. Toast until the bread is crisp and golden brown and the filling is heated through, 5–10 minutes. Serve hot.

Caramelized onion jam has a delicious sweet and savory flavor that goes beautifully with cheese and bread. You can buy it in most supermarkets, but do try our simple recipe on page 42. Try it with other panini in this chapter; add a layer to the Roasted Apple & Cheese Panini on page 34, or substitute it for the chutney in the Sourdough Cheese & Chutney Panini on page 35.

CHEESE & CARAMELIZED ONION panini

8   slices whole-wheat (wholemeal) bread or walnut bread

4   tablespoons (60 g) melted butter

About $^1/_2$ cup (120 g) caramelized onion jam, storebought or homemade (see page 42)

5   ounces (150 g) Brie or Camembert cheese, thinly sliced

Serves 4 • Preparation 10 minutes • Cooking 5–10 minutes • Difficulty 1

1. Preheat a sandwich toaster or panini press on medium-high heat.

2. Brush one side of each slice of bread with a thin layer of melted butter.

3. Set out four slices of bread, butter-side down. Spread with a layer of caramelized onion jam followed by a layer of cheese. Top with the remaining slices of bread, butter-side up.

4. Toast until the bread is crisp and golden brown and the cheese is melted, 5–10 minutes. Serve hot.

If you liked this recipe, you will love these as well.

FIG, PANCETTA & GOAT CHEESE panini

CHEESE, CUMIN & GOLDEN RAISIN panini

ROASTED APPLE & CHEESE panini

PESTO

Makes about 2 cups (500 ml) • Preparation 10 minutes
Difficulty 1

½	cup (90 g) pine nuts, lightly toasted	1	cup (250 ml) extra-virgin olive oil
2	cloves garlic, coarsely chopped	5	cups (250 g) basil leaves
½	cup (60 g) coarsely grated Parmesan cheese		Salt and freshly ground black pepper

1. Place the pine nuts and garlic in a food processor and blend to make a coarse paste.

2. Add the cheese and half the oil and blend to combine. Add the basil leaves and pulse, stopping to scrape down the sides occasionally, until blended.

3. Gradually add the remaining oil and blend until a paste is formed. Season with salt and pepper.

4. Use immediately or store in an airtight container in the refrigerator for 4–5 days.

MAYONNAISE

Makes about 1½ cups (370 ml) • Preparation 15 minutes
Difficulty 1

2	large egg yolks		vinegar
2	teaspoons Dijon mustard	1	cup (250 ml) extra-virgin extra-virgin olive oil
1	tablespoon freshly squeezed lemon juice		Salt and freshly ground white pepper
1	tablespoon white-wine		

1. Place the egg yolks, mustard, lemon juice, and vinegar in a medium bowl and whisk to combine. Gradually add 3 tablespoons of the oil, whisking continuously until incorporated.

2. Add the remaining oil in a thin, steady trickle, whisking until thick and creamy. Season with salt and pepper.

3. Store in an airtight container in the refrigerator for 2–3 days.

CARAMELIZED onion jam

Makes about 3 cups (750 ml) • Preparation 10 minutes
+ 12 hours to cool • Cooking 60–75 minutes • Difficulty 1

3	tablespoons extra-virgin olive oil	¾	cup (180 ml) malt vinegar
2	pounds (1 kg), white onions, thinly sliced	2	tablespoons seeded (wholegrain) mustard
1	cup (200 g) firmly packed light brown sugar	1	teaspoon finely grated orange zest
		3	juniper berries, cracked

1. Heat the oil in a medium heavy-based saucepan over low heat. Add the onions, stir to coat, then simmer, stirring frequently, until caramelized, 30–45 minutes.

2. Add all the remaining ingredients, stir to combine, and bring to a boil. Decrease the heat to low and gently simmer, stirring frequently, until thick and sticky, about 30 minutes.

3. Spoon the jam into sterilized glass jars and seal. Leave to cool overnight before serving. Store in the refrigerator for up to 2 months.

TOMATO chutney

Makes about 5 cups (1.25 liters) • Preparation 30 minutes
+ 12 hours to cool • Cooking 90 minutes • Difficulty 1

4½	pounds (2 kg) green tomatoes, chopped		raisins (sultanas)
3	onions, chopped	4	small dried red chiles, finely chopped
3	tart green cooking apples, peeled, cored, and chopped	3	bay leaves
1½	cups (375 ml) cider vinegar	2	teaspoons salt
1½	cups (300 g) sugar	2	teaspoons black mustard seeds
⅓	cup (60 g) golden	1	teaspoon black peppercorns
		1	teaspoon whole cloves

1. Put the green tomatoes, onions, apples, cider vinegar, and sugar in a large heavy-based saucepan over medium heat. Stir and simmer until the sugar has dissolved. Add the golden raisins, chiles, bay leaves, salt, and mustard seeds and stir to combine.

2. Put the peppercorns and cloves on a small piece of muslin. Tie with kitchen string to make a spice bag. Add to the pot and simmer, stirring frequently, until thick, about 1½ hours.

3. Spoon into sterilized glass jars and seal. Leave to cool overnight before serving. Store in a cool, dark place for up to two months. Refrigerate after opening.

SUGAR & SPICE panini

4	tablespoons light brown sugar
$\frac{1}{2}$	teaspoon ground cinnamon
$\frac{1}{2}$	teaspoon ground ginger
$\frac{1}{4}$	teaspoon ground nutmeg
	Pinch of ground cloves
2	tablespoons melted butter
1	small banana, thinly sliced
2-3	tablespoons slivered almonds
4	slices white or brown sandwich bread

Serves 2 • Preparation 10 minutes • Cooking 5–10 minutes • Difficulty 1

1. Preheat a sandwich toaster or panini press on medium-high heat.

2. Mix the sugar, cinnamon, ginger, nutmeg, and cloves in a small bowl.

3. Brush one side of each slice of bread with a thin layer of melted butter. Top two slices of bread with the banana. Sprinkle with the almonds and sweet spice mixture. Cover with the remaining slices of bread. Trim off the crusts.

4. Toast until the bread is crisp and golden brown, 5–10 minutes. Cut each panino in half on the diagonal to make triangles. Serve hot.

NUTELLA & ALMOND panini

½ cup (120 g) chocolate hazelnut spread, such as Nutella

2–3 tablespoons slivered almonds

4 slices white sandwich bread

Serves 2 • Preparation 10 minutes • Cooking 5–10 minutes • Difficulty 1

1. Preheat a sandwich toaster or panini press on medium-high heat.

2. Spread the chocolate hazelnut spread on two slices of bread. Sprinkle with the almonds. Cover with the remaining slices of bread. Trim off the crusts.

3. Toast until the bread is crisp and golden brown, 5–10 minutes. Cut each panino in half on the diagonal to make triangles. Serve hot.

wraps

BLT wraps

4	large flour tortillas
8	slices bacon, rinds removed
2	tomatoes, seeded and chopped
1	avocado, pitted and chopped
2	scallions (green onions), chopped
2	cups (100 g) mixed salad greens
$1/2$	cup (125 g) mayonnaise, storebought or homemade (see page 42)
1	tablespoon Dijon mustard
1	(3-ounce/90-g) package cream cheese, softened

Serves 4 • Preparation 20 minutes • Cooking 5 minutes • Difficulty 1

1. Wrap the tortillas in barely damp double layers of paper towels and microwave on high for 45 seconds. Alternatively, warm them in an ungreased frying pan over medium heat.

2. Heat a large frying pan over medium heat. Add the bacon and sauté until crisp and golden brown, about 5 minutes. Crumble into a medium bowl.

3. Add the tomatoes, avocado, scallions, and salad greens to the bowl. Mix the mayonnaise and mustard in a small bowl then add to the bowl with the bacon mixture. Toss well.

4. Spread some of the softened cream cheese on each warm tortilla. Spread the bacon mixture on top and roll up. Serve immediately.

If you liked this recipe, you will love these as well.

CHICKEN & BELL PEPPER wraps

CHEESE, SALAMI & ARUGULA wraps

TURKEY & AVOCADO wraps

SWEET & SPICY CHICKEN wraps

panini, wraps & sandwiches wraps 48

4	Lebanese flat breads, pita breads, or flour tortillas
4	cups (400 g) shredded cooked chicken
1/2	cup (120 ml) mayonnaise, storebought or homemade (see page 42)
2	tablespoons sweet chile sauce, storebought or homemade (see page 10)
1	cucumber, thinly sliced
2	tomatoes, chopped
1	large carrot, finely grated
2	cups (100 g) finely shredded lettuce
	Salt and freshly ground black pepper

Serves 4 • Preparation 10 minutes • Cooking 5–10 minutes • Difficulty 1

1. Wrap the flat breads in barely damp double layers of paper towels and microwave on high for 45 seconds. Alternatively, warm them in an ungreased frying pan over medium heat.

2. Mix the chicken, mayonnaise, and sweet chile sauce in a large clean bowl.

3. Lay the flat breads out on a clean surface. Divide the chicken mixture, cucumber, tomatoes, carrot, and lettuce evenly among them. Season with salt and pepper. Roll up and cut each wrap in half. Serve while still warm.

CHICKEN & BELL PEPPER wraps

Spice Mix

2	teaspoons dried oregano
1	teaspoon sweet paprika
1	teaspoon ground cumin
1	teaspoon onion powder
1	teaspoon garlic powder
1	teaspoon sea salt
$1/2$	teaspoon ground chipotle (Mexican chile powder)

Wraps

$1^{1}/4$	pounds (600 g) chicken thigh fillets, skin off
3	tablespoons (45 ml) extra-virgin olive oil + extra to drizzle
1	red bell pepper (capsicum)
1	green bell pepper (capsicum)
1	large onion, thinly sliced
8	flour tortillas
1	cup (250 ml) guacamole, storebought or homemade (see page 52)
$1/2$	cup (125 g) sour cream

Serves 4–8 • Preparation 10 minutes + 12 hours to chill • Cooking 5–10 minutes • Difficulty 2

Spice Mix

1. Combine all the spice mix ingredients in a small bowl.

Wraps

1. Combine the chicken, oil, and spice mix in a medium bowl and toss to coat. Cover and refrigerate overnight.

2. Preheat a chargrill on high heat and a flat-grill on medium heat. Chargrill the bell peppers until the skins are blistered and blackened. Place in a bowl, cover with plastic wrap (cling film), and set aside for 10 minutes. Remove the skins.

3. Drizzle a little oil onto the flat plate. Cook the onion until softened and golden brown. Chargrill the chicken until cooked through, 4–5 minutes each side. Slice into thin strips.

4. Wrap the tortillas in barely damp double layers of paper towels and microwave on high for 45 seconds. Alternatively, warm them in an ungreased frying pan over medium heat.

5. Spread a layer of guacamole on each tortilla. Top with bell peppers, sour cream, and chicken. Roll up and serve warm.

Wraps are rolled sandwiches made by wrapping wheat-flour tortillas, or other flat breads such as pita bread, lavash, or naan, around some sandwich ingredients. They are very similar to tacos and burritos and were probably inspired by these Mexican classics. Many wraps, including the one on this page, are spread with guacamole, a classic Mexican dip or sauce made from mashed avocados seasoned with salt, chiles, garlic, and lime juice.

SHRIMP & PINEAPPLE WRAPS with guacamole

2	large flour tortillas
8	medium shrimp tails, shelled and deveined
2	slices fresh or canned pineapple, chopped
1/2	cup (120 g) storebought or homemade guacamole (see page 52)
2	tablespoons finely chopped fresh cilantro (coriander)
	Salt and freshly ground black pepper

Serves 2 • Preparation 10 minutes • Cooking 3–5 minutes • Difficulty 1

1. Wrap the tortillas in barely damp double layers of paper towels and microwave on high for 45 seconds. Alternatively, warm them in an ungreased frying pan over medium heat.

2. Combine the shrimp and pineapple in a preheated grill pan over high heat and cook, turning often, until the shrimp is pink and cooked through, 3–5 minutes.

3. Spread the tortillas with guacamole and top with the shrimp and pineapple. Sprinkle with the cilantro.

4. Season with salt and pepper. Roll up and serve warm.

If you liked this recipe, you will love these as well.

SALMON & CREAM CHEESE wraps

TUNA & PESTO wraps

SHRIMP & AVOCADO rolls

GUACAMOLE

Makes about 2 cups (500 ml) • Preparation 10-15 minutes
Difficulty 1

2	avocados, halved lengthwise and pit removed	1/2	green birds' eye chile, seeded and finely chopped
2	tablespoons freshly squeezed lime juice		Salt and freshly ground black pepper
1	clove garlic, chopped		Dash of Tabasco sauce
2	scallions (spring onions), thinly sliced		

1. Use a teaspoon to remove the flesh from one avocado and place in a food processor with the lime juice and garlic. Blend until smooth. Transfer to a medium bowl.

2. Peel and dice the remaining avocado and add to the puréed mixture. Add the scallions and chile and stir to combine. Season with salt, pepper, and Tabasco sauce.

3. Serve immediately or on the day of making.

HUMMUS

Makes about 3 cups (750 ml) • Preparation 15 minutes
+ 12 hours • Cooking 1 hour • Difficulty 1

1	cup (200 g) dried garbanzo beans (chick peas), soaked in cold water overnight	3	tablespoons tahini paste
1/3	cup (90 ml) extra-virgin olive oil	3	cloves garlic, coarsely chopped
1/4	cup (60 ml) freshly squeezed lemon juice	3	teaspoons ground cumin
			Salt

1. Drain and rinse the garbanzo beans. Place in a medium saucepan, cover with cold water, and bring to a boil. Decrease the heat and simmer until tender, about 1 hour. Drain, reserving 1/2 cup (125 ml) of the cooking liquid.

2. Place the garbanzo beans, oil, lemon juice, tahini, garlic, and cumin in a food processor and blend to make a coarse paste. Gradually add the reserved cooking liquid, blending to make a smooth paste. Season with salt.

3. Use immediately or store in an airtight container in the refrigerator for 4-5 days.

PINEAPPLE salsa

Makes about 4 cups (1 liter) • Preparation 15 minutes
Difficulty 1

1/2	fresh pineapple, peeled, cored and cut into 2/3-inch (1.5-cm) dice	2	tablespoons freshly squeezed lime juice
1/2	cup (15 g) coarsely chopped fresh cilantro (coriander)	1	tablespoon Thai fish sauce
2	red birds' eye chiles, seeded and finely chopped	2	teaspoons finely grated jaggery (palm sugar) or light brown sugar
2	tablespoons roasted peanuts, coarsely chopped	1	teaspoon finely grated ginger
		1	teaspoon sesame oil

1. Combine the pineapple, cilantro, chiles, and peanuts in a medium bowl.

2. Combine the lime juice, fish sauce, jaggery, ginger, and oil in a small bowl and stir until the jaggery has dissolved.

3. Pour the lime juice mixture over the pineapple mixture and toss to combine.

4. Use immediately or store in an airtight container in the refrigerator for 2-3 days.

MANGO salsa

Makes about 4 cups (1 liter) • Preparation 15 minutes
Difficulty 1

2	ripe mangos	1	tablespoon white rum
2	scallions (spring onions), thinly sliced	1	teaspoon sugar
1/4	cup fresh mint leaves, torn		Freshly ground black pepper
	Freshly squeezed juice of 2 limes		

1. Cut the mangos either side of the pit creating two cheeks. Peel and cut the flesh into 2/3-inch (1.5-cm) dice. Dice any remaining flesh, discarding the pit.

2. Combine the mangos, scallions, and mint in a medium bowl.

3. Put the lime juice, rum, and sugar in a small bowl and stir until sugar dissolves. Pour over the mango mixture and toss to combine. Season with pepper.

4. Use immediately or store in an airtight container in the refrigerator for 2-3 days

CHEESE, SALAMI & ARUGULA wraps

panini, wraps & sandwiches wraps

54

2   piadinas (Italian flat breads) or large flour tortillas

4   ounces (120 g) stracchino cheese (or cream cheese)

2   ounces (60 g) thinly sliced spicy salami

Small bunch arugula (rocket)

Salt and freshly ground black pepper

2   tablespoons extra-virgin olive oil

Serves 2 • Preparation 10 minutes • Cooking 5 minutes • Difficulty 1

1. Wrap the piadinas or tortillas in barely damp double layers of paper towels and microwave on high for 45 seconds. Alternatively, heat them in an ungreased frying pan over medium heat.

2. Spread with the cheese, Top with the salami and arugula. Season with salt and pepper and drizzle with the oil.

3. Roll up and serve warm.

SPINACH & PROVOLONE WRAPS with pesto

4   large whole-wheat flour tortillas

$^3/_4$ cup (180 ml) sour cream

$^1/_4$ cup (60 ml) pesto, storebought or homemade (see page 42)

1   cup (50 g) packed fresh spinach leaves, tough stems removed, torn

1   large tomato, thinly sliced, cut in half

4   large slices provolone cheese, cut in half

    Freshly grated black pepper

Serves 4 • Preparation 10 minutes • Cooking 5 minutes • Difficulty 1

1. Wrap the tortillas in barely damp double layers of paper towels and microwave on high for 45 seconds. Alternatively, heat them in an ungreased frying pan over medium heat.

2. Mix the sour cream and pesto in a small bowl. Spread the sour cream mixture evenly over the tortillas. Top with the spinach leaves, tomatoes, and cheese. Season with pepper.

3. Roll up and serve warm.

Ranch dressing was invented by Steve Henson in the 1950s on the Hidden Valley dude ranch he and his wife owned near Santa Barbara, California. The dressing became so popular that the couple began to bottle and sell it to their guests. In 1972 they sold the brand to Clorox, which still makes the dressing (along with many other companies).

56

TURKEY & AVOCADO wraps

Ranch Dressing
2	cloves garlic
1/2	teaspoon salt
1	cup (250 ml) storebought or homemade mayonnaise (see page 42)
1/4	cup (60 ml) buttermilk or sour cream
2	tablespoons finely chopped fresh parsley
2	tablespoons finely chopped fresh chives
1	scallion (green onion), thinly sliced
1	teaspoon white wine vinegar
	Freshly ground black pepper

Wraps
12	slices bacon, rinds removed
4	large flour tortillas
1	cup (50 g) mixed baby salad greens
12	ounces (350 g) sliced roast turkey breast
1	medium-large tomato, sliced
1	avocado, peeled, pitted and sliced
2	teaspoons freshly squeezed lime juice
	Salt and freshly ground black pepper
1	cup (50 g) watercress

Serves 4 • Preparation 20 minutes • Cooking 5 minutes • Difficulty 1

Ranch Dressing
1. Mash the garlic and salt with the side of a chef's knife. Whisk the garlic, mayonnaise, buttermilk, parsley, chives, scallion, vinegar, and pepper in a medium bowl. Use immediately or cover and refrigerate for up to 3 days.

Wraps
1. Heat a frying pan over medium heat. Sauté the bacon until crisp and golden brown, 3–5 minutes. Drain on paper towels.

2. Wrap the tortillas in barely damp double layers of paper towels and microwave on high for 45 seconds. Alternatively, heat them in an ungreased frying pan over medium heat.

3. Top the tortillas with salad greens followed by the turkey, bacon, tomato, and avocado. Drizzle with the lemon juice. Season with salt and pepper. Top with the watercress and drizzle with Ranch Dressing. Roll up and serve immediately.

If you liked this recipe, you will love these as well.

TURKEY, BELL PEPPER & HAZELNUT panini

TURKEY, BLUE CHEESE & CRANBERRY wraps

TURKEY bagels

GREEK PITA wraps

½ cup (120 ml) mayonnaise, storebought or homemade (see page 42)

1 tablespoon freshly squeezed lemon juice

1 sweet red onion, finely chopped

1½ cups (400 g) canned garbanzo beans (chick peas), drained and rinsed

1 cooked chicken breast, about 5 ounces (150 g), thinly sliced

4 ounces (120 g) feta cheese, crumbled

1 small green bell pepper, seeded and chopped

2 tomatoes, chopped

1 cup (200 g) tzatziki, storebought or homemade (see page 88)

6 large crisp lettuce leaves

6 pita breads

Serves 6 • Preparation 10 minutes • Cooking 5–10 minutes • Difficulty 1

1. Combine the mayonnaise, lemon juice, onion, and garbanzo beans in a medium bowl. Mix well, mashing the beans slightly with fork. Stir in chicken, feta, bell pepper, and tomatoes.

2. Soften the pita breads by wrapping in paper towels and microwaving on high for about 1 minute. Alternatively wrap in a damp kitchen towel and place in the oven at about 300°F (150°C/gas 2) for 5–10 minutes.

3. Place a lettuce leaf on each pita bread. Top with the filling and spoon some tzatziki over the top. Roll up and serve immediately.

CHARD & CHEESE wraps

2   tablespoons extra-virgin olive oil
1   large onion, sliced
3   cloves garlic, finely chopped
1   tablespoon red pepper flakes
½   cup (125 ml) chicken stock
1   bunch Swiss chard (silverbeet), tough stems removed and coarsely chopped
     Salt
8   small corn tortillas
1   cup (150 g) queso fresco or ricotta cheese
1   cup (200 g) tomato salsa, storebought or homemade (see page 88)

Serves 4 • Preparation 10 minutes • Cooking 15–20 minutes • Difficulty 1

1. Heat the oil in a frying pan over medium heat. Add the onion and sauté until softened, 3–4 minutes. Add the garlic and red pepper flakes, stirring until fragrant, about 1 minute.

2. Stir in the chicken stock, Swiss chard, and salt. Cover and simmer over low heat until the chard is nearly tender, about 5 minutes. Remove lid and increase heat to medium, stirring until the liquid evaporates, about 5 minutes. Remove from heat and set aside.

3. Wrap the tortillas in barely damp double layers of paper towels and microwave on high for 45 seconds. Alternatively, heat them in an ungreased frying pan over medium heat.

4. Spread the tortillas with the chard, and top with the cheese and salsa. Roll up and serve warm.

These wraps make a light and healthy lunch. Use leftover roast chicken or turkey if you have it on hand.

CALIFORNIA CHICKEN & BLUE CHEESE wraps

Chicken Breasts

2	boneless skinless chicken breasts
1	large onion, chopped
2	carrots, chopped
2	bay leaves
1	teaspoon whole black peppercorns
2	tablespoons white wine vinegar
	Salt

Wraps

8	slices bacon, rinds removed
4	large flour tortillas
$1/2$	cup (125 ml) mayonnaise, storebought or homemade (see page 42)
5	ounces (150 g) blue cheese, at room temperature
1	avocado, pitted and sliced
	Crisp romaine lettuce leaves

Serves 4 • Preparation 20 minutes • Cooking 20–25 minutes • Difficulty 1

Chicken Breasts

1. Put the chicken breasts in a medium saucepan with enough cold water to cover. Add the onion, carrots, bay leaves, peppercorns, and vinegar and bring to a boil. Season with salt. Cover and poach until tender and white, about 15 minutes. Drain well, discarding the vegetables.

Wraps

1. Heat a frying pan over medium heat. Sauté the bacon until crisp and golden brown, 3–5 minutes. Drain on paper towels.

2. Wrap the tortillas in barely damp double layers of paper towels and microwave on high for 45 seconds. Alternatively, heat them in an ungreased frying pan over medium heat.

3. Spread with mayonnaise and sprinkle with blue cheese. Thinly slice the chicken breasts and place on top. Cover with bacon, avocado, and lettuce. Roll up and serve warm.

If you liked this recipe, you will love these as well.

CHICKEN, CELERY & PISTACHIO panini

CHICKEN, SLAW & PAPAYA wraps

CHILE, CHICKEN & CARROT wraps

TANDOORI CHICKEN & YOGURT wraps

62

2   tablespoons tandoori paste
1   cup (250 g) plain yogurt
8   chicken tenderloins, about 1 pound (500 g)
2   tablespoons finely chopped fresh mint leaves
1   cup (50 g) baby spinach leaves
4   chapati breads or large flour tortillas

Serves 2 • Preparation 15 minutes + 30 minutes to chill • Cooking 5–10 minutes • Difficulty 1

1. Combine the tandoori paste and $1/2$ cup (120 ml) yogurt in a shallow glass or ceramic bowl. Add the chicken. Toss to coat. Cover and chill in the refrigerator for 30 minutes.

2. Preheat a barbecue plate or chargrill over medium-high heat. Cook the chicken until browned and cooked through, 3–5 minutes each side.

3. Combine the mint and remaining $1/2$ cup (120 ml) yogurt in a bowl. Wrap the chapati or tortillas in barely damp double layers of paper towels and microwave on high for 45 seconds. Alternatively, heat them on the barbecue or grill.

4. Spread the spinach, chicken, and yogurt mixture along the center of each wrap. Roll up and serve warm.

CHICKEN, SLAW & PAPAYA wraps

1/4 head each red and green cabbage, finely shredded

1/2 cup (25 g) finely chopped fresh cilantro (coriander)

4 scallions (green onions), sliced

2 tablespoons habanero hot sauce

Freshly squeezed juice of 1 orange

Freshly squeezed juice of 1 lime

2 tablespoons sesame oil

8 ounces (250 g) boneless skinless chicken breast, poached and julienned (see page 60 for poaching instructions)

1 ripe papaya, peeled and sliced

4 large flour tortillas

Serves 4 • Preparation 15 minutes • Cooking 15–20 minutes • Difficulty 1

1. Combine the cabbage, cilantro, and scallions in a bowl and toss. Add hot sauce, orange and lime juices, and sesame oil. Mix thoroughly. Add chicken and toss well.

2. Wrap the tortillas in barely damp double layers of paper towels and microwave on high for 45 seconds. Alternatively, heat them in an ungreased frying pan over medium heat.

3. Spread each tortilla with some of the chicken mixture and top with some papaya. Roll up and serve warm.

These sliced wraps make a pretty addition to a buffet spread. They need to be chilled in the refrigerator for an hour to become firm enough to slice. Remove from the refrigerator and slice about 10 minutes before serving.

SALMON & CREAM CHEESE wraps

1 cup (250 g) cream cheese, at room temperature

1/2 cup (25 g) finely chopped fresh mixed herbs: chives, dill, and scallions + extra to garnish

1 medium cucumber

8 ounces (250 g) smoked salmon, sliced thinly

8 large flour tortillas

Serves 8 • Preparation 20 minutes + 1 hour to chill • Difficulty 1

1. Mix the cream cheese and herbs in a small bowl and set aside. Slice the cucumber very thinly lengthwise using a mandolin or very sharp knife.

2. Wrap the tortillas in barely damp double layers of paper towels and microwave on high for 45 seconds. Alternatively, heat them in an ungreased frying pan over medium heat.

3. Spread the tortillas with a layer of the cream cheese mixture. Top with a layer of cucumber slices followed by a layer of salmon slices. Roll up.

4. Place seam-side down on a plate and cover with plastic wrap (cling film). Chill in the refrigerator for 1 hour.

5. Cut in 2-inch (5-cm) slices, discarding the uneven ends. Sprinkle the serving dish with a few extra fresh herbs and arrange the wraps on top.

If you liked this recipe, you will love these as well.

105

SALMON, MASCARPONE & LIME rolls

106

ROBIOLA & SMOKED SALMON rolls

119

SALMON FLOWER sandwiches

SAUSAGE & TABBOULEH wraps

Tabbouleh

1/3	cup (90 g) fine- or medium-grain bulgur
1	cup (50 g) finely chopped fresh parsley
2	tablespoons finely chopped fresh mint
1	large tomato, finely chopped
1/2	small red onion, finely chopped
1	tablespoon extra-virgin olive oil
1/4	cup (60 ml) freshly squeezed lemon juice
	Salt and freshly ground black pepper

Wraps

6	spicy sausages, such as pepperoni
1	tablespoon extra-virgin olive oil
4	Lebanese flat breads, pita breads, or flour wraps
2/3	cup (150 g) hummus, storebought or homemade (see page 52)

Serves 4 • Preparation 40 minutes • Cooking 15 minutes • Difficulty 1

Tabbouleh

1. Put the bulgur in a bowl and cover with cold water. Let stand for 30 minutes.

2. Squeeze out the excess moisture and transfer to a bowl. Stir in the parsley, mint, tomato, onion, oil, and lemon juice. Season with salt and pepper.

Wraps

1. Sauté the sausages in the oil in a large frying pan over medium heat until cooked, 5–10 minutes. Remove from the heat and cut into long thick slices.

2. Wrap the flat breads in barely damp double layers of paper towels and microwave on high for 45 seconds. Alternatively, heat them in an ungreased frying pan over medium heat.

3. Spread evenly with the hummus and top with the tabbouleh and sausage. Roll up carefully. Cut each wrap in half and serve.

HAM & BEAN wraps

$^{1}/_{2}$ cup (125 g) canned red kidney beans, drained and rinsed

$^{1}/_{2}$ cup (75 g) canned corn kernels, drained

1 medium tomato, chopped

1 medium avocado, chopped

1 tablespoon sweet chile sauce, storebought or homemade (see page 10)

4 large wheat tortillas

8 slices ham

$^{1}/_{2}$ cup (75 g) freshly grated tasty Cheddar cheese

Serves 4 • Preparation 10 minutes • Difficulty 1

1. Combine the beans, corn, tomato, avocado, and chile sauce in a bowl.

2. Wrap the tortillas in barely damp double layers of paper towels and microwave on high for 45 seconds. Alternatively, heat them in an ungreased frying pan over medium heat.

3. Spread the tortillas with the ham, bean mixture, and cheese. Roll up and serve warm.

Lamb, hummus, tabbouleh, olive oil, lemons: this wrap has all the best flavors of the eastern Mediterranean land of Lebanon.

LEBANESE LAMB wraps

¹⁄₄ cup (60 ml) extra-virgin olive oil

1 clove garlic, crushed

2 tablespoons freshly squeezed lemon juice

¹⁄₂ teaspoon dried mixed herbs

Salt and cracked black pepper

1 pound (500 g) lamb backstraps, trimmed

4 Lebanese flat breads or pita bread

1 cup (250 g) hummus, storebought or homemade (see page 52)

1 cup tabbouleh (see page 66)

Serves 4 • Preparation 20 minutes + 30 minutes to chill • Cooking 10–15 minutes • Difficulty 2

1. Combine the oil, garlic, lemon juice, mixed herbs, salt and pepper in a non-metallic bowl and mix until well combined. Add the lamb and toss until evenly coated. Cover and refrigerate for 30 minutes.

2. Heat an indoor grill or barbecue hot plate to high heat. Drain the lamb from the marinade. Grill until cooked to your liking, about 5–7 minutes each side. Set aside to rest for 5 minutes.

3. Wrap the flat breads in barely damp double layers of paper towels and microwave on high for 45 seconds. Alternatively, heat in a large ungreased frying pan over medium heat.

4. Slice the lamb. Spread the flat breads with hummus and top with tabbouleh and lamb. Roll up and serve warm.

If you liked this recipe, you will love these as well.

PLOUGHMAN'S wraps

MEDITERRANEAN ROAST BEEF wraps

MEATBALL & BABA GANOUSH wraps

PLOUGHMAN'S wraps

2   Lebanese flat breads or large flour tortillas

$^1/_2$ cup (120 g) tomato or fruit chutney, storebought or homemade (see page 42)

$^1/_2$ cup (25 g) freshly grated tasty Cheddar cheese

4   thin slices roast beef

$^1/_2$ cup (25 g) mixed baby salad greens

1   large tomato, diced

Serves 2 • Preparation 5–10 minutes • Difficulty 1

1. Wrap the flat breads in barely damp double layers of paper towels and microwave on high for 45 seconds. Alternatively, heat in a large ungreased frying pan over medium heat.

2. Spread evenly with the chutney. Sprinkle with the Cheddar. Top with the roast beef, salad greens, and tomato. Roll up and serve warm.

MEDITERRANEAN ROAST BEEF *wraps*

4   pieces wholemeal lavash
2   cups (500 ml) hummus, storebought or homemade (see page 52)
8   thin slices roast beef
1   cup (200 g) semidried tomatoes, chopped
1   bunch arugula (rocket)

Serves 4 • Preparation 5–10 minutes • Difficulty 1

1. Wrap the lavash in barely damp double layers of paper towels and microwave on high for 45 seconds. Alternatively, heat in a large ungreased frying pan over medium heat.

2. Spread evenly with the hummus and top with roast beef, semidried tomatoes, and arugula. Roll up and serve warm.

Lavash is a soft, thin flat bread from Armenia, Georgia, and Iran.
It is idea for wraps.

CHILE, CHICKEN & CARROT wraps

2	pieces lavash bread or large flour tortillas
2	cups (250 g) leftover shredded roast chicken
2	tablespoons sweet chile sauce, storebought or homemade (see page 10)
1	cup (25 g) shredded romaine (cos) lettuce
1	carrot, coarsely grated

Serves 2 • Preparation 10 minutes • Difficulty 1

1. Wrap the lavash in barely damp double layers of paper towels and microwave on high for 45 seconds. Alternatively, heat in a large ungreased frying pan over medium heat.

2. Combine the chicken and chile sauce in a bowl.

3. Spread the chicken mixture, shredded lettuce, and carrot over the lavash bread. Roll up and serve warm.

If you liked this recipe, you will love these as well.

28

CHICKEN, FETA
& PESTO panini

32

HOT STUFF CHICKEN
SOURDOUGH panini

76

CHICKEN WRAPS with
pesto & sundried tomatoes

FALAFEL & SALAD wraps

4   Lebanese flat breads or pita breads

1   head romaine lettuce, sliced

2   tomatoes, sliced

1   small sweet red onion, sliced

1   red bell pepper (capsicum), seeded and sliced

½   cup (120 ml mayonnaise, storebought or homemade (see page 42)

8–12   falafel (see page 88)

Serves 4 • Preparation 20 minutes + 2 hours to rest • Cooking 15 minutes • Difficulty 1

1. **Wrap** the flat breads in barely damp double layers of paper towels and microwave on high for 45 seconds. Alternatively, heat them in an ungreased frying pan over medium heat.

2. **Spread** the flat breads with mayonnaise and cover with the lettuce. Top with the tomatoes, onion, bell peppers, and falafel. Roll up and serve warm.

MEATBALL & BABA GANOUSH wraps

1 tablespoon ground cumin
1 1/2 pounds (750 g) lean ground (minced) beef
1 red onion, finely grated
1/2 cup (35 g) bread crumbs made from day-old bread
2 fresh red birdseye's chiles, seeded and finely chopped
1/4 cup coarsely chopped fresh cilantro (coriander) leaves
1 large egg, lightly beaten
Salt and freshly ground black pepper
1/4 cup (60 ml) vegetable oil
1 bunch arugula (rocket)
1 bunch fresh mint, leaves picked
1/2 bunch fresh cilantro (coriander)
8 large flour tortillas
1 cup (250 g) baba ganoush (see page 88)
1 (8-ounce/250 g) jar or bottle roasted bell peppers (capsicums), drained

Serves 6 • Preparation 20 minutes • Cooking 40 minutes • Difficulty 1

1. Combine the cumin, beef, onion, bread crumbs, chilies, chopped cilantro and egg in a large bowl. Season with salt and pepper. Mix well. Roll into balls and flatten slightly to form 2-inch (5-cm) patties (you should get about 24).

2. Heat 1 tablespoon of oil in a large frying pan over medium-high heat. Cook about 10 patties for 2 minutes each side or until cooked through. Drain on paper towels. Repeat with remaining oil and patties in 2 batches.

3. Toss the arugula, mint, and extra cilantro in a bowl.

4. Wrap the tortillas in barely damp double layers of paper towels and microwave on high for 45 seconds. Alternatively, heat them in an ungreased frying pan over medium heat.

5. Spread the tortillas with baba ganoush. Cover with the arugula mixture and bell peppers. Top with the patties and roll up. Serve warm.

CHICKEN WRAPS with pesto & sundried tomatoes

1 cup (150 g) plain couscous
1 clove garlic, peeled
2 cups (100 g) fresh basil leaves
3 tablespoons (45 ml) extra-virgin olive oil
1/4 teaspoon salt
1/8 teaspoon freshly ground pepper
1/2 cup (60 g) freshly grated Parmesan cheese
1/2 cup (60 g) coarsely chopped walnuts
4 large flour tortillas
3 cups (350 g) shredded cooked chicken
16 sundried tomato halves packed in oil, drained and coarsely chopped
1 yellow bell pepper (capsicum), cored, seeded, and diced

Serves 4 • Preparation 20 minutes • Cooking 5–10 minutes • Difficulty 1

1. Prepare the couscous according to the instructions on the package. Set aside.

2. Combine the garlic, basil, oil, salt, and pepper in a blender. Blend well until smooth. Stir in the cheese.

3. Toast the walnuts in a small frying pan over medium heat, 3–5 minutes. Set aside.

4. Wrap the tortillas in barely damp double layers of paper towels and microwave on high for 45 seconds. Alternatively, heat them in an ungreased frying pan over medium heat.

5. Spread each tortilla evenly with basil pesto, couscous, chicken, walnuts, sundried tomatoes, and bell peppers. Roll up and serve warm.

FALAFEL & HUMMUS wraps

4	multigrain or plain flour tortillas
1/2	cup (120 g) hummus, storebought or homemade (see page 52)
1/2	baby cos lettuce, leaves separated, torn
1	cup (150 g) tabbouleh (see page 66)
1	cucumber, sliced lengthwise into long ribbons
8-12	falafel, storebought or homemade (see page 88)

Serves 4 • Preparation 10 minutes • Difficulty 1

1. Wrap the tortillas in barely damp double layers of paper towels and microwave on high for 45 seconds. Alternatively, heat them in an ungreased frying pan over medium heat.

2. Spread the tortillas with hummus. Top with lettuce, tabbouleh, cucumber, and falafel. Roll up and serve warm.